MW00357027

1 MONTH OF
FREE
READING

at

www.ForgottenBooks.com

By purchasing this book you are eligible for one month membership to ForgottenBooks.com, giving you unlimited access to our entire collection of over 1,000,000 titles via our web site and mobile apps.

To claim your free month visit:

www.forgottenbooks.com/free818582

ISBN 978-0-331-13447-6
PIBN 10818582

the public affairs committee

This pamphlet is one of a series published by the Public Affairs Committee, a nonprofit educational organization founded in 1935 "to develop new techniques to educate the American public on vital economic and social problems and to issue concise and interesting pamphlets dealing with such problems."

Maxwell S. Stewart, Editor

Mabel C. Mount, Managing Editor

Copyright, 1951, by the Public Affairs Committee, Inc. Ninth Edition, July, 1961.

 64

Mrs. Neisser, formerly a group leader for the Association for Family Living, is now Child Guidance editor for Childcraft. Mrs. Neisser is co-author, with her husband, of the Public Affairs Pamphlet, Making the Grade as Dad. She is a grandmother.

A KINDERGARTEN teacher was singing a song to her little charges about dear grandma, and how we like to bring her a shawl as she sits by the fire. Suddenly, she noticed the pert, fortyish grandmother of one of her pupils standing in the doorway.

"Of course, boys and girls, you understand this song is about great-grandmothers," she added hastily.

Shawls and fireplaces are scarcely characteristic of either the equipment or the habitat of grandmothers or of mothers-in-law today. This notion is thoroughly out of date. Mothers-in-law, grandmothers, and even great-grandmothers are not likely to be dear little old ladies. They are much more apt to be alert, vigorous women with plenty of ideas and energy. They have the assurance gained in raising their own families and coping with a world which has gone from magic lantern slides to television.

why she differs from the stereotype

There are at least three forces that have combined to make a woman who is in her forties, fifties, or sixties today different from the picture built up by earlier generations. First, medical science has made it possible for her to stay younger and healthier physically, and public opinion requires that she take advantage of what medicine offers. The ailing lady languishing on the sofa is out of tune with the times and gets scant sympathy.

Second, the manners and the demands of life today make it necessary for a woman to pay attention, to be up-to-date, not to be too rigidly set in her ways. For better or for worse, the cult of youth has a firm hold on us here in America. "Mother" is judged by her ability to keep up in appearance, tastes, and vitality with her daughters and daughters-in-law.

She cannot stay in one spot in her attitudes and ideas, or even geographically. The odds are her children will be scattered over the country. If she wants to visit them, if she must live now with one, now with another, or if she answers the urgent summons to lend a hand in emergencies, she must be willing to pick up and go where they are. The number of middle-aged, to say nothing of elderly, women traveling by themselves on cross-country busses, transcontinental coach planes, and through trains shows how much she does pick herself up and go.

Finally, the stylists and the cosmeticians have played no small part in bringing about the change. As a result of frequenting bargain basements as well as exclusive salons, a woman in middle life can have becoming, appropriate clothes and a figure, hair-do, and face that conceal her age. Unlike the lady in Gilbert and Sullivan's *Trial by Jury* who "could easily pass for forty-three in the dusk with a light behind her," the woman with married children today could do so in the full glare of high noon or Kleig lights.

All these factors combine to make her feel younger than she would have felt at the same age two or three or even one generation ago, and as a result, her goals have changed. Whether she is a wife or a widow, she is not of a mind to live in the past. She is aware that she could not, even if she wanted to, play the dowager queen to her family. She wants to have an active part in the life around her.

What is she to do then? It may be helpful to take stock of the position of a mother-in-law and grandmother today and ask:

2

What are some of the inherent difficulties in being a mother-in-law, and what attitudes make the relationship pleasanter?
What can a grandmother contribute to her grandchildren?
What does she need in order to do her job well, and what solutions are available to her?

her position today

A woman in middle life, whose children are married, is to some extent out of the job she has held for twenty-five or thirty years. There may still be some young people at home, but the size of the family has shrunk enough to make a noticeable difference in the housekeeping. Smaller quarters may be in order for Mother and Father. Simplified living has its pleasant side, but to a certain extent it leaves a woman unemployed emotionally and practically. A husband can take up some of the emotional slack, but too much hovering isn't good for him either.

Today many women who are widows must also make the adjustment to mother-in-law and being grandmother. This makes for a more serious kind of emotional unemployment.

Another complicating force in the life of the woman who is assuming these new roles may be her justifiable anxiety about the menopause which she may be going through. As a result, she may be temporarily less confident, less poised, less eager to make the effort to meet new situations. She is troubled too by such questions as: Will her married children welcome her in their homes? Or will they have the resentment many people harbor toward mothers-in-law? Perhaps they will repeat the pattern of feelings she has known only too well about her own mother-in-law. Each of us wants to have a close, warm, friendly relationship with our married children, and at the same time to be the exceptional mother and mother-in-law who is never in the way. Can it be done?

THE HAZARDS OF BEING A MOTHER-IN-LAW

In a recent contest for the loveliest mother, held by a metropolitan newspaper, a picture came in accompanied by this note: "Here is a picture of my wife's mother. In spite of the fact that she is my mother-in-law, I think she is tops."

3

Mothers-in-law have had such a bad press that a man feels he has to apologize for thinking his wife's mother an admirable woman. When such an attitude about a relationship has become traditional, one naturally asks: *Is there something in the relationship itself which creates difficulties, regardless of the behavior of the individuals involved?* The answer is: *Yes.* Inescapable pulls and tensions are part and parcel of your feelings toward the people your children marry, and of their feelings toward you.

The way the relationship is handled by both generations can aggravate or reduce the tension, but there are four reasons why you may be resented as a mother-in-law even though your conduct is flawless.

First, sometimes you are the ideal which a daughter-in-law feels she can never attain. The pies that Mother used to bake are a symbol. The actual quality of those pies is not the point at issue. In moments of stress or discouragement, sons are likely to paint a glorified picture of Mother and her ways, overlooking the very human disagreements they may frequently have had with that same mother.

Sometimes, for a daughter-in-law, the mother of her husband actually *is* stiff competition. Take what happened to young Ruth Elliott when she married and came to River City. The senior Mrs. Elliott was a by-word for friendliness, not only in her own circle but among all those who served her.

Every time Ruth set foot in a store, visited the dentist, or went to the post-office, she heard some variation on the theme, "Oh, so you're the Elliotts' daughter-in-law. Mrs. Elliott certainly is a wonderful woman. Wish there were more like her."

It seemed to shy, self-conscious Ruth, that everyone was making unfavorable comparisons between her mother-in-law's graciousness and her own arkwardness. The phantom ideal that disturbs many young wives was a reality in her case. In her anxiety over the competition the older woman seemed to present, Ruth actually rebuffed her mother-in-law pretty rudely.

put the blame on mom

Second, in contrast to the above, many a husband or wife may feel that his or her mate was never understood or appreciated as a child. He or she may therefore be angry with the parents-in-law who "never gave Jim (or Jenny) the break he (or she) deserved."

4

A third reason for irritation is that wives and husbands tend to lay the blame for all a spouse's shortcomings on mother-in-law.

"If you'd had any training at home, you'd know that a husband shouldn't be late for dinner every night."

"If your mother had brought you up right, you'd be able to get along on what I make."

These gibes may or may not be good-natured, but underlying them is the feeling that if his (or her) mother had known her business, he (or she) would be easier to live with now.

Finally, a mother-in-law may be a scapegoat. Perhaps your son-in-law or daughter-in-law has often been angry at his or her own mother, but has felt guilty about that anger and pushed it out of the way. Disliking one's own mother is not an acceptable sentiment, but annoyance at a mother-in-law stamps no one as a heartless, ungrateful creature. The unacceptable feelings are transferred to *you*, as another member of the same sex and same generation who stands in a similar position.

the people your children marry

In the same way, there are opposing and unconscious pulls and tensions in your attitude toward the people your children marry. Three different feelings may disturb you. In the first place, grown children represent a tremendous emotional investment. As a result, you are not always enraptured with the people they marry.

Then, too, because you have given yourself so fully to watching over and guiding your children for many years, it is hard to believe that this green girl, one step beyond a bobby-soxer, or that callow youth who never before has taken much responsibility, is qualified for the important task of looking after your son or your daughter and before long, your grandchildren.

How often we hear, "Of course, I want Kate to get married. It's just that I don't believe Charlie is grown up enough to look after her. If they'd only wait a year or two . . ."

5

In the third place, you may actually find yourself with a son-in-law or daughter-in-law whose ideas, standards, and values are different from your own. Manners, tastes, and interests may offer little common ground for establishing a cosy, comfortable intimacy. Trivial matters bulk so large in any close relationship that it would probably be easier to have a son-in-law who was a pirate than one who disagrees with you about radio comedians; how well a steak should be done; or whether little boys should quit the ball game to greet their grandmothers even when the bases are loaded.

Owing to all of these feelings which at some times, to some degree, probably are present in most people, your relationship to your grown children and their partners is not only a matter of what is said and done today. It is shaped at different times by different feelings of long standing. You need not, therefore, feel you are being personally insulted by a cross word, a black look, or even a more serious outburst. Not what you say or do, *but what you symbolize* is frequently the root of the difficulty.

REDUCING THE TENSION

In spite of the unavoidable resentments, there are some steps that go far toward making the relationship with sons-in-law and daughters-in-law more satisfactory. Without being unduly optimistic, you can hope to find a pleasant experience in a close friendship with an agreeable younger woman who shares your good opinion of your son. As for sons-in-law, it can happen that a lively young man will bring new points of view, new interests into your life.

What are some attitudes that have proved constructive in creating mutual friendliness and respect between two generations in day-to-day living? There are many, and different approaches will work best in different families. But here are nine points it may be well to consider.

1. Both generations have to be flexible

No rules can be laid down about the deference due to age or the right of younger people to go their own way; about your right to demand attention, or about being completely independent and accepting no favors.

Situations can only be worked out, difficulties resolved, through compromises. Sometimes you may be the one to offer care, other times you may be the one to be cared for. If you can do both with good grace, everyone concerned will be happier.

Mrs. Martin was determined not to inconvenience her children. Because she insisted on being everlastingly self-effacing and self-sacrificing, she ended by being just as tiresome as if she had always insisted on carrying out her own wishes, and she was discontented besides.

It took a cheery, easy-going friend to show her that there was a better way of getting on with married children and their families.

"My daughters-in-law know I'll put myself out for them if I can, and they aren't afraid to ask me to pitch in when they need me," her friend explained. "But last winter when I had the flu, why, I just had to ask for help. 'I know I'm going to be a nuisance whether I like it or not,' I told them, 'But once I get out of this mess, I'm going to send each of you off on a spree while I take over for you.' They know I'll speak up if I want another piece of pie, or if I have some plans of my own when they want me to baby-sit, or whatever. It's giving sometimes, and taking sometimes, I always say . . . and we make out pretty well that way."

2. they have a right to make their own decisions

If your objective is to meet your grown children and their mates on a footing of friendly equality rather than trying to control them — even for what appears to be for their own good — you will acknowledge their right to make the important decisions in their lives. Where they shall live, how they shall spend their money or their leisure, how they shall divide their responsibilities, are all personal matters every couple must work out for themselves.

Carrie, a story by Huston Macready that appeared in *Harper's Magazine* in 1931, was an excellent illustration of how much sorrow well-intentioned managing can bring. A young couple returned from their wedding trip to find that the parents of the groom were presenting them with a house completely furnished down to the last bedspread and lampshade. The house, though sturdy and well laid out, was totally without charm and not in the least like the house Caroline, the bride, had dreamed of.

At the end of the story you know that all her hopes for a good marriage have died, and the gay, spirited Caroline must become "Carrie," the submissive daughter-in-law, at least until such time as she leaves her husband altogether.

Rose Franken's play, *Another Language*, which deals with a mother who tries to control her sons and their wives, shows another kind of domination. The mother and one of her daughters-in-law, are discussing the behavior of another daughter-in-law.

HELEN: *Wasn't it last year she wanted to take a job or something?*

MRS. HALLAM: (Exercised) *Yes, and it was all I could do to make Victor put his foot down. "Victor," I told him, "your wife doesn't have to support you. It's more important for her to make you a good home and bear your children."*

3. regard them as a unit

Any mother who makes her son put his foot down is heading for real trouble. The first loyalty of every man or woman is to his wife or her husband. As a mother-in-law you reinforce that loyalty every time you think of the couple as a unit, every time you speak to them, or write to them, or talk about them as "Harriet and Steve" rather than "My son Steve, and his wife Harriet."

8

The corollary to this principle is that you never say anything to either one you would not be willing to say to both, for make no mistake, sooner or later the other one will hear about it. When a son or daughter marries, it is hard to realize that you will never again communicate with him or with her as your child, but always as half of a husband-and-wife combination.

Because they are a unit, you fare better if you can avoid taking sides in their quarrels. As one seasoned mother-in-law put it, "When an argument starts, I take a walk. Then I don't know what happened, and I am not pulled in."

4. it's against the rules to stir up trouble

Mrs. Perkins occasionally became annoyed at her son-in-law, Pete, because she felt he was inconsiderate of his wife, Joan. Then she would tell her daughter, "If I were you, I wouldn't stand for it. You don't have to be a doormat."

Joan loved Pete enough to overlook some of the things that irked her mother. True, there were times when she took a stand about something that really mattered to her, but of those incidents Mrs. Perkins knew nothing. Yet when her mother reproached her for being a spineless creature, Joan began to doubt herself. Then she grew angry at her mother for planting such doubts, and usually ended up by reporting the whole episode to her husband who in turn was outraged at his mother-in-law's interference.

Inciting rebellion or creating bad feelings should be against the principles of all right-thinking mothers-in-law. There is all the difference in the world between stating your own disapproval mildly, for superhuman self-control is not required of anyone, and trying to persuade a wife or husband that he or she should not endure such treatment.

5. accept them as they are

"I could do so much for Marianne, if she would just let me," Mrs. Tucker often told her husband. Marianne, the wife of their son, Paul, did not run her little flat or entertain her friends in what Mrs. Tucker considered "suitable fashion."

"I told her I'd gladly lend her my best tablecloth and my good china when she has Paul's crowd and their wives. And just imagine,

9

she said she thought. nobody's appetite would be spoiled by paper plates. Paper plates for company!"

It was hard for Mrs. Tucker to understand that Marianne saw in her mother-in-law's well-intentioned offers a reflection on her own way of doing things, and therefore bristled at every suggestion.

A much wiser woman was Mrs. Corbetti. She had recently returned from a stay at her son's home where she had been keeping things going while the younger Mrs. C. went to the hospital to have a third baby.

"I'll bet you housecleaned like mad while you were there. These young girls don't seem to mind how thick the dust gets," one of her friends remarked.

"That's just what I didn't do," answered Mrs. Corbetti. "I'll admit Nancy isn't a raging housekeeper, but she's darling with those youngsters of hers, and Fred adores her. She had put everything in what *she* thought was apple-pie order before I came. If I'd turned the house inside out according to my notions of how it should be, it would have been as good as telling her I didn't like the way she did things. I went there to look after Fred and the little boys, and I left her closets and cupboards strictly alone."

6. go easy with suggestions

To say that a mother-in-law should never give advice or make suggestions would be to take all the spontaneity out of her contacts with her married children. Many times a frank expression of feeling can clear the air. Still, it is a good idea to watch how, to whom, and how often you volunteer your opinions. Advice, like any commodity, is more sought after when it is scarce and hard to get. But where you feel you must make suggestions, you might start by saying, "Do you think this might be a good idea?"

It takes time and patience to discover where you must tread lightly and where the fabric of the relationship can stand some strain. It may be a good plan to ration your critical comments and directions. Reserve your ammunition for the really important matters rather than keeping up a barrage of "Of course I wouldn't interfere for the world, but if I were you, etc., etc."

It is not a question of putting your plan across, but of what putting that plan across will do to the relationship.

10

7. discretion pays off

Nobody enjoys hearing how well somebody else disciplines his children, manages his income or chooses her hats. Your sons and daughters and their mates will appreciate your good judgment in not reporting the successes or failures of one household to another. The fact that you are not a carrier of gossip not only makes them enjoy your company more, but it makes them feel it is safe to confide in you.

They especially value your restraint in not discussing Billy's sniffles or Nell's tantrums with your casual friends.

8. share responsibilities when you live together

No grown woman relishes having any other woman permanently in her kitchen as a volunteer. We all prefer being in business for ourselves domestically, even when an extra pair of hands is a real help. The feelings of two women who are engaged in a joint housekeeping project are likely to be mixed. Much as each may appreciate the other's assistance, inevitably and at the same moment, each tends to resent the other, although the resentment may be pushed out of sight most of the time.

11

No two people make a bed, clean a sink, or peel a potato in exactly the same way, yet there are innumerable good ways of doing these things. If two generations who must live together realize this, they can usually plan a division of duties in keeping with the time, the energy, and the skill which each has to contribute.

When Mrs. Soderstrom came to live with her son and daughter-in-law, she was treated almost as a guest, rather than as a member of the family. She never felt comfortable in her daughter-in-law's kitchen, and when she did lend a hand there, she would ask hesitatingly, "Is this the way you want it, Sylvia?" or go into long explanations to justify her own way.

After a month or two, both women realized that they were on the wrong track. They made a fresh start and decided that each of them would have definite jobs to do daily and weekly. It was agreed that each would do her own job in her own way and at her own pace while recognizing that there was more than one right way to do it.

In some families where the younger woman works outside the home, a further step has been taken with satisfactory results. The older woman takes over the running of the household, and by mutual consent this job is acknowledged to merit a modest wage. The whole matter then is on a more self-respecting and business-like basis. The mother-in-law does not feel either that she is being a burden or that she is being overworked.

9. accept the fact that you are an in-law

The two mothers of a married couple may compete for the affection and good opinion or perhaps the control of the younger people. This is particularly apt to happen where there are grandchildren. Sometimes it is hard to accept the fact that, no matter how devoted you have been, a daughter-in-law or son-in-law turns to her or to his own people in a crisis. If you do understand this, you may avoid an unfortunate kind of competition.

Almost before you have had time to become accustomed to thinking of yourself as a mother-in-law, another new relationship presents itself. It has often been said that the best reason for having children is in order to have grandchildren, but even in being a grandparent there are a few tense moments.

12

BEING A GRANDMOTHER

One of the difficulties that confront a grandmother is only a continuation of the problem of being a mother-in-law. Two people who are separated in age by twenty or thirty years, are bound to have different points of view. The gap between three generations is greater still. You have had more experience in living and are undoubtedly wiser; yet along with wisdom, age and experience have brought a degree of caution.

When eight-year-old Ned and his friends build a tree house, you recall all the broken bones you ever heard of that resulted from small boys' falling out of such precarious roosts. Possibly you forget that the four broken collar bones that come to your mind are counterbalanced over a period of fifty years by all the small fry who had the time of their lives in tree huts.

All manner of adventures may look more dangerous to you just because you yourself would not be overjoyed at climbing a shaky ladder, plunging into cold water, or driving three hundred and fifty miles in a day. There is in everyone at times a slight trace of the feeling that prompted a certain grandmother to say to her ten-year-old granddaughter, "Betsy, how *can* you eat any more? I'm not the least bit hungry; you'd better stop."

On the other hand, age and experience have made it possible for you to take the more tolerant, long-term view when younger heads may have become embroiled in the perplexities of the moment. You can afford to smile when your son or son-in-law declares he won't stand for such behavior from a six-year-old, and what is the world coming to if little girls talk back to their fathers like that?

You may remember all too well how six-year-olds — perhaps the very ones who, now grown, are so full of moral indignation — talked back to mothers and fathers without causing the heavens to fall. Grandparents do not *always* have to keep still at such moments. But compared with the number of times you express your point of view, the number of times you keep quiet probably seem without number.

In some respects, being a grandparent may have been more satisfactory a few generations ago when Grandma was looked to as the Voice of Experience on matters of health, household management, and child training. But no matter how up-to-date you may have been in the care of your own family, new discoveries coming out of scientific research have changed the thinking in many fields. These advances cannot be dismissed as fads or theories. They are the best knowledge at present available. Another twenty years may see them superseded by still other practices, but the fact that we do not have final answers is no reason for not making use of the best we have.

GRANDMOTHER'S CONTRIBUTION

In spite of these difficulties, this is a good era in which to be a grandmother, for there is general agreement that no expert can ever

take away the essential contribution grandparents can make in furthering the development of their grandchildren.

Today it is acknowledged that no children can have too much of the right kind of love. Grandparents are needed to add a greater measure of that priceless ingredient of emotional health.

Since grandparents are traditionally and often unjustly accused of spoiling the young, it may be helpful to examine the difference between the kind of love that helps a child grow and the kind that spoils him. The right kind of love enjoys the baby, the runabout youngster, the school boy or girl, even the teen-ager *as he is*. It welcomes the fact that some day he will grow up, and assures him that growing up is worth the effort.

Spoiling might be defined as denying the child the right to use his powers to practice independence and self-reliance on the one hand, or, on the other hand, insisting he meet standards that are too high for him.

It is a great relief to many parents as well as grandparents to discover that this important matter of loving a child consists largely of enjoying him as he is with the warmth and spontaneity that are natural to most people who are grown up in their feelings.

Grandparents also help a child's emotional development by widening the circle in which children feel at home. The first thing a baby learns — if he is well cared for — is that his mother and his father are people whom he can trust. He has discovered they keep him fed and warm and comfortable, but as for the rest of the world, who knows?

It is a fortunate baby or toddler who has a chance to discover that Grandma's arms can be just as comforting as Mother's. This astonishing discovery gives him courage to trust other people, too, and lays the foundation for a sense of security. A little later, playing, eating, and sleeping at Grandma's give him the feeling that he can be safe and happy away from home base. Grandparents are the best introduction to the world-away-from-home.

Grandmother's house often stands for the chance to have a friendly sympathetic. adult all to one's self away from brothers and sisters who make competition tough. Even getting away from parents who may be cracking down in such matters as language, bathing, or doing the dishes, may be a relief. Every human being needs to escape from the demands of daily life once in a while. If Junior at four or six or eight years of age finds Grandmother's house a place of refuge, more power to him — and to her!

children need to learn to be flexible

The small child soon finds out there is a difference between the way Grandma does things and the way Mother does things. Grandma does not like doors slammed, while Mother does not seem to mind minor noises. Cookies between meals are taboo in Mother's book, but Grandma doesn't think a cookie ever goes amiss. Just as often, it is the other way around.

Does this confuse the small child? Usually not. Of course, a situation in which a youngster of any age continually plays his parents off against his grandparents, is definitely undesirable. Short of that, children learn a vital lesson when they discover that there is more than one way to be tucked in bed or to season spinach.

Three-year-old Linda had remarked a dozen times during the first days of her visit with her grandparents, "Mommee doesn't do that way," or "Mommee says, 'do like this.' "

15

Mrs. Rigert found herself growing a little annoyed at the implied criticism in Linda's voice, but all she said was, "That's a nice way, too, but this is how we do it here."

The little girl looked thoughtful, but said nothing. After a few days, Mrs. Rigert heard Linda talking to her doll. "Grandma's house, so you take a nap in bed, Dolly. Our house, you take naps on the couch. That's the way it is."

grandparents can foster a sense of belonging

The older generation makes a contribution in widening the horizon of a child's mind as well as his feelings. The three-year-old likes stories about himself as a baby. The five-year-old delights in hearing about his parents when they were small, particularly about their pranks and misdemeanors. "Tell me about the longest ago you remember," was the frequent request of one seven-year-old.

Sometimes in an effort not to live in the past, grandparents overlook the wealth of possibilities for enriching young people's understanding of the world. Not only stories of your own youth, but stories you in turn may have heard from your own parents and grandparents can be a source of pleasure to the grandchildren. Such stories can give them a sense of having roots and belonging and can give the past real meaning.

It is true that comparisons in favor of the good old days are tiresome, but colorful and lively accounts of those times can be one of your unique contributions to your grandchildren.

grandmother is indispensable on a practical level

A mother with several small children can barely manage the cooking, cleaning, and mothering that she is called upon to do in the course of each twenty-four hours. No automatic machinery can take the place of an extra pair of hands in an emergency, and that extra pair of hands is likely to be Grandma's.

know how much you can give

How much of your time and strength go into helping out is something you have to decide for yourself on the basis of the other demands you must meet, and the energy you have available. There are no union rules for grandmothers, nor is what the neighbors may say a suitable yardstick. You have to be sufficiently self-confident and self-respecting to know how much you can give before such giving becomes a drain on you. Both you and your children, and even the grandchildren, will feel better about the help you offer if you are frank about telling them when it is impossible for you to drop everything and constitute yourself a rescue party.

she makes a contribution to her grown children, too

We may discount some of the sentimental songs about mothers, but the fact remains that even the most self-reliant of our children occasionally face moments when some encouragement from Mother can save the day. Even sons-in-law and daughters-in-law sometimes find the moral support of an interested, older person heartening.

If at such moments you are a good listener; slow to blame and ready to look for ways of unraveling a tangled situation; able to take a "this isn't the first time such things have happened" point of view, you will probably be offering helpful counsel.

Grandmothers, then, are invaluable for the love, the security, the flexibility, and the sense of belonging they can bring to their grand-children. The practical assistance as well as the moral support they can provide to their own grown children are a part of their contribution, too.

PRINCIPLES OF CHILD GUIDANCE

In order to do the job of being a grandmother well (and it also helps in the mother-in-law situation), you need an understanding of present-day principles of child development.

If you have devoted a lifetime to bringing up your own family, why do you need to make a deliberate effort to understand current ideas about bringing up youngsters? Certainly it is not because you are lacking in common sense or experience, but if you turn your back on the new principles, which your grandchildren's parents subscribe to, then "modern child psychology" can become a source of conflict between the generations. And it is one source of conflict you can avoid.

There is no mystery about the principles of modern child guidance. Don't let any high-flown talk about child psychology throw you.

17

Don't let anybody tell you, "Mother, you just can't understand the new ways." Changes in theory, swings of the pendulum, newer ways, all boil down to these few points.

In 1920 or 1930 when you were bringing up your own children, you undoubtedly relied on habit training to make them into well-behaved youngsters. It was taken for granted by almost everyone that if you drilled a child in desirable habits by continual repetition, rewarding satisfactory performance and punishing unsatisfactory behavior, you would have a creditable child. The earlier you started the better, for you mustn't let a youngster get away with anything. A child must not be allowed to question parental authority, nor must he be allowed to get a good opinion of himself lest he get the upper hand.

What has happened in the last twenty or thirty years? As a result of observations made on thousands of children, doctors, educators, and students of human development discovered some new facts about the way children grow. Present-day recommendations to parents are based on these facts.

children want to grow up

The drill theory overlooked one vital point: children are not like pieces of clay to be pounded and pressed into the desired shape. They are more like plants that have within them a strong drive to grow. This holds true for growth in feelings and the ability to get along with people, as well as bodily growth. Plants need, in addition to good soil and light, a gardener who cooperates with growth and occasionally does some pruning or staking so that a plant will not run wild all over the lot like a weed.

We know now that children want more than anything else in the world to grow up and to imitate the parents who love them and whose love they return. Youngsters learn how to behave, not through everlasting drill or an elaborate system of reward and punishment, but because they want to do what the adults around them do. They try not only to imitate the actions of the grown-ups but their parents' feelings, too.

In order to learn, to develop in mind, in feelings, in ability to get along with others, a child needs to like himself. The happy, self-confident child may sometimes be mischievous, often be noisy or get dirty, or be less than mannerly and punctual, but he is not likely to be the one who is seriously destructive, steadily angry, or constantly doing things to provoke the adults.

they need to feel protected

Parents and grandparents do need to set limits on what children may do. Friendly firmness on the part of Mother and Father makes a child feel safe, safe even from what he fears he might do. The happy child knows there are many things he may do, and some few he may not do. He will occasionally do something that is wrong, for conscience develops slowly; but the boy or girl who conforms because he feels cooperative most of the time is learning to get along with others and to be independent.

Today's friendly firmness, with encouragement to the effect that "Johnny will do better next time . . . Johnny is the kind of little boy who will grow up . . . He is O.K., even though he did get into trouble this afternoon," is different from the old idea that child guidance is a battle to demonstrate who's boss. Children know all too well that adults are big and powerful. Much of their misbehavior stems from their fear of what these giants may do to them or a misinterpretation of what the giants want them to do.

different kinds of control at different stages

Every child has to go through certain phases as he grows. It is our job, as guiding adults, to give children the opportunity to take new steps as they are ready. Here lies the answer to those who are concerned lest the indulgence granted to babies will be continued in late childhood. It is true that babies are fed when they are hungry, and

19

comforted when they cry, these days. They are allowed to establish their own rhythm of eating and sleeping, and usually it turns out to be a sensible rhythm. Being permitted complete gratification in babyhood makes it *more*, not *less* possible for them to accept restrictions later on. They have learned to trust their mothers. The ability to endure waiting for satisfaction grows through the years if there has been enough gratification in infancy.

There was a brief period about twenty-five years ago when a few educators experimented with unlimited freedom for children of all ages. The only people who benefited from this unbridled license were the cartoonists. They had a wonderful time ridiculing those who submitted to the despotism of their children.

Present-day child guidance need not be a bogey-man to grandparents. Rather than emphasizing repetition with attendant reward and punishment, the best thinking today advocates guidance that cooperates with growth in offering opportunities to go on to each new step as the child is ready. It recognizes that children need different amounts and different kinds of control at different times in their lives. Our children are not trying to get the best of us. The more real self-respect and self-confidence they have, the happier they will be and the easier they will be to live with.

GRANDMOTHER'S CODE

If there were a Union of Amalgamated Grandmothers, it might have a three-point code for its members.

Unless you must take care of your grandchildren day after day in the absence of their own mother, it is the parents rather than you who have the final responsibility for them. In a democracy, he who must take the responsibility for a job is usually granted the privilege of regulating that undertaking. It is to the parents rather than to the grandparents that custom today in America accords the final word on how children shall be raised.

Although each generation profits by the mistakes of the preceding one, still it will make other mistakes of its own. It is hard to stand by and watch parents, particularly young parents, go forward on a course that seems likely to end in misfortune, if not downright catastrophe. But it is comforting to remember that while each generation will err in a different direction, the mistakes of one will tend to be not much more serious than the mistakes made by its predecessors.

As a grandmother, you have many advantages over a mere parent. You may be less hurried and harassed. You may have your grandchildren with you one at a time so that the difficulty of being fair to two or three or even four simultaneously in the matter of affection and attention does not present itself. Because you do not have a steady and exclusive diet of the company of young children, you may relish it more than their mother does. Most of all, just because you are less weighed down with the feeling of responsibility and because you are more mature, you can very often enjoy the company of your grandchildren in a more relaxed mood than their own parents can.

It would be unfair, however, to use your advantage in an attempt to come first with your grandsons and granddaughters. They may tell you at times that they like you better than Mommy or Daddy, and as long as you do not take this statement too seriously there is no harm in it.

You will be on safe ground as long as you keep in mind the fact that just as the first loyalty of your son or daughter is to the family he or she is founding, so should the continuing loyalty of a child be first of all to its parents rather than to its grandparents. His trust in his parents' kindness and competence is the source of his security, his faith in life itself.

It would be against the code of ethical grandmothers to try to come between a youngster and his mother or father. Now, all small boys and girls love secrets and conspiracies. Especially delightful are secrets with Grandma involving that extra portion of ice cream; or a surprise for Mother in the form of the amazing news that five-year-old Cindy has learned to tie a bow; or a promised picnic come the first warm Saturday. Such delicious conspiracies are a source of joy to young and old, and hurt no one. Only a pact which you in your own mind would not be willing to have the youngster's parents' know about, or one whose purpose it is to draw a small person closer to you *at the expense of his loyalty to his mother or father,* would be unfair competition.

Mrs. Brockway and her granddaughter

Roger Angell's story, *Summer in the Mountains,* which appeared in the *New Yorker* in May, 1949, is a subtle illustration of this kind of competition. The story concerns Mrs. Brockway and her grand-daughter, Jane Porter. Between Mrs. Brockway and her daughter, the mother of Jane, there exists deep but unspoken tension. The older woman is lonely and feels excluded from the Porters' lives in spite of their correct kindness to her.

Mrs. Brockway has been left with Jane for the evening. She has been reading the little girl a story, and there is a sense of cozy warmth between them. It occurred to Mrs. Brockway that if she could have Jane to herself for a little while she could regain that sense of being loved and needed which would assuage her loneliness. She suggested to Jane that it would be fun if the two of them were to go away for a trip together, perhaps this summer, and she gave the little girl a nostalgic account of the place in the mountains where she and Jane's mother used to spend their vacations. Jane went along with the plan until her grandmother suggested that this be kept a secret between them; she was doubtful about anything that must be hidden from her mother.

Carried away by the idea of reliving her years as the mother of a small girl, Mrs. Brockway suggested that perhaps she and Jane might even go away for a little trip at Christmas time. This was too much for Jane. The suggestion that she should leave her parents for Christmas was downright frightening, and she burst into tears.

Mrs. Brockway herself was alarmed at what she had done. Most alarming to her was the expression on Jane's face which told her that instead of drawing the little girl closer to her, she had only succeeded in undermining her confidence in her grandmother. How could Jane trust someone who sought to divide her loyalties? So Mrs. Brockway's scheme to ease her own feeling of isolation defeated its purpose, and left her more cut off from those she loved.

It is hard to realize that, no matter how happy the grandchildren may be with you, their own Mom and Dad are still the center and the core of their world and in our society that is best for them.

being a grandmother is not a career

This code for grandmothers, like the attitudes that have been recommended for mothers-in-law, may seem to imply that success and satisfaction in both roles lies more in what you refrain from saying or doing than in what you actually do. Indeed, it is good to have a certain detachment, the kind that is vividly described in that current colloquialism, "stay loose."

If you can stay loose, if you can avoid becoming too involved in the lives of your grandchildren and their parents, you can make of grandmotherhood a fascinating hobby, a splendid avocation. That is just what it should be. For being a grandmother is not a career. But if you attain that detachment, you might be in danger of finding yourself in a vacuum. In order to resolve this dilemma, everyone needs an interest—something you do because you like to do it, not because you have to. Everyone needs some enterprise, or cause, or affiliation outside herself and her family. Such an interest is a necessity, at least until you are ready to be like the eighty-eight-year-old heroine of V. Sackville West's *All Passion Spent* for whom "the only things that touched reality were the routine of her life and the growth of her bodily ailments, for which she was beginning to feel quite an affection."

Since grandmothers may be any age upward of forty, they will choose to use their energy and time in a wide variety of ways. Here it is possible to indicate only a few of the avenues to explore in search of satisfying interests.

You may be lucky enough to have some pursuit which you enjoyed either as an amateur or perhaps professionally in your younger days which you can pick up again now that you have time. What you may have lost in dexterity through the years is more than made up for by the greater maturity you bring to the activity now.

For the woman who lives with her son and daughter, and must depend on them for support, some money of her own is a boost to her self-respect as well as a practical help. An untrained woman over

23

forty may not readily find a paying job in business or industry, but she may have resources within herself that she has never suspected.

jobs after forty

There are, in some communities, exchanges for women's work that specialize in selling homemade delicacies and fine hand-sewn articles such as baby clothes and lingerie. Your Chamber of Commerce or Better Business Bureau could probably tell you if there is an opportunity of this kind in your town.

New York State has a woman Deputy Commissioner of the State Department of Commerce who assists women who want to market some products they make. This is not an employment bureau, but an advisory service for women who want to set up their own business on a small scale. Most of the 11,000 women who have been helped to start small businesses of their own in the last six years since the program started, are over thirty-five. Theirs is a success story, but not on the grand scale. Nobody expects them to turn the baking of cookies or the making of scarfs into a factory operation, but many of them clear around $500 a year on enterprises carried on in their own homes.

Maine has started a state agency similar to the one in New York, and California has been holding clinics for women who want advice before starting a venture. Women's groups in other states are working toward similar services. Your State Commissioner of Labor in the state capitol, or your local Chamber of Commerce would be able to tell you if there is anything like this service near you.

There is no reason why high-school girls should have a corner on the baby-sitting market. Most parents would rather have a mature woman who has brought up a family of her own. Sitters are always at a premium, especially during the daytime hours. You would probably not have to do much more than let it be known through the backyard grapevine that your services are available, and you would be in business—although in many places baby-sitter guilds are proving helpful.

Assuming that she does not have to earn her living in a full-time job, how is she to supplement the place her children and grandchildren hold in her life in order to round it out, to make it fuller and richer?

24

Many women are finding that for the first time in their lives, after their children are grown and married, they have a chance to pursue interests of their own. It is not too late to learn a new skill. Almost every community offers some kind of adult education at a nominal cost, often at no cost at all. Such an adult education program usually includes some of the arts and crafts. Have you always thought it might be fun to weave or to get your hands on some clay, just to see what you could do with it? Have you ever wondered what it would feel like to try painting, or whether making designs for linoleum block printing was as much fun as it looked? You can start now.

Community centers or boards of education would be the places to find out what kind of facilities are available in your neighborhood. Often, just talking about an idea leads to the discovery of other people who want to do the same thing or of someone who can help you get started.

You may be surprised to find how many of the men and women who are attending informal groups to acquire new skills or get new ideas, are like yourself, over forty.

grandmothers are needed in the community

Many women find making a contribution to the life of the community satisfying too. Welfare, civic, and political organizations are clamoring for volunteers. If you would like to help in a community service organization, but don't know how to get started, and if you live in a city of over twenty-five or thirty thousand inhabitants, look in the telephone book for the Council of Social Agencies, or Welfare Council. Such an organization acts as a clearinghouse for all the health and welfare agencies in town. It would be the center for information on what kind of volunteer work the hospitals, the clinics, old people's homes, the orphanages or child placement agencies, the Scouts, the Y's, the settlements, the family service societies and the Red Cross need. A volunteer job might be anything from escorting crippled children from one part of the hospital to another, to doing simple office work or reading to a blind person. The Welfare Council can usually direct you to the places where you can get more detailed descriptions of the jobs that need to be done and the qualifications for them.

Don't be discouraged if you promise to do something and it turns out to be quite humdrum. It is not just what you do that may make the difference between flatness and flavor in your own life. The contacts you make, the new interests that open up to you as you stay with the work are important too, and if you are reliable and cheerful, promotions can even come to a volunteer.

Friends are important, too

Perhaps you would like to find a few congenial friends. You may have moved to a new community or lost touch with old acquaintances. In order to provide older people with companionship, many neighborhood centers and churches have set up Golden Age Clubs where men and women can find a pleasant social life with others whose tastes are similar. Your church, your Neighborhood Center, or the Welfare Council if you live in a city large enough to have one, would probably know about the activities for seniors, or about the possibilities for getting such activities under way.

If you are interested in the fascinating but puzzling political questions of the day on a local or national level you would probably find the program of the League of Women Voters appealing. Because in many cities this program is centered around neighborhood discussion groups, it is a good way to become acquainted with your neighbors, as well as an excellent way to gain an understanding of your community.

In rural areas, the County Extension Service of the State Department of Agriculture would probably be able to tell you if any such organizations exist near your home.

You do not need to limit yourself to Golden Age Circles—indeed, you may not be old enough to qualify! This country is so full of clubs of every possible kind that you are pretty sure to find some group that would interest you and welcome you as a member. There is no need to be shy about making inquiries. The Young Women's Christian Association, if there is one in your community, has women's groups for all ages. Church Guilds and Auxiliaries are not to be overlooked. Then there are the women's auxiliaries to many of the men's fraternal or labor groups which may be open to you because of your husband's affiliation. In many communities a Co-ordinating Council maintains a list of all the groups that meet regularly and have an active program. A call to that Council would give you a clue as to what is afoot in your vicinity.

The essential matter is to find and maintain an interest in some activity, whether it be a craft, a community service, a money-making venture, or an organization whose purpose is educational or social. Curiously enough, once you acquire such an interest, you, yourself, become a more vital and more stimulating person. You are less concerned with small annoyances that may have been causing friction between you and your sons and daughters, their mates, your grandchildren, and even your husband. Rather than feeling you are neglecting them for some kind of gadding about, they will have a better opinion of you. If your company is a little hard to get because you spend two afternoons a week at the Red Cross or the Altar Guild, or doing baby sitting, your presence will be more highly valued.

it all adds up

Being a mother-in-law and grandmother and liking it, depends chiefly on your attitudes toward your grown children, their wives and husbands, and your grandchildren. There are certain difficulties inherent in the relationship that can probably never be completely overcome, but with an awareness of those hazards, it is possible through what you say and do to reduce and prevent some tension.

Your relationship with your children and grandchildren will tend to go more smoothly and to be richer if you do not rely solely on them for gratification. No one can live entirely and constantly through others and stay happy and healthy emotionally. An exclusive diet of self-sacrifice leads to emotional malnutrition just as surely as would a steady diet of having other people make sacrifices for you. Taking part with people outside your family in some undertaking that seems worthy of effort and attention is not a luxury or a frill. It is almost a necessity if life is to be lived with any zest or relish.

face to the future

It is not always easy to remember that the faces of the next generation are set toward the future—whether that future looks bright or not. If you can keep your face in that direction, too, then you have a better chance of marching along with those you love best, of not being left behind, and of finding satisfaction in "the last of life for which the first was made."

173

N416

C.

acksl
Health Work
ability
ir

.

ial?
ophy

against Disease
l Health
ms
llout
ce in Cancer
Not Myths
iuse

dren

"our Life
bled

le
ir Business
our Family
Arteries
roblems

Can be Beaten

ie Epileptic

ins

:h

.

ND - #0150 - 051222 - C0 - 229/152/2 [4] - CB - 9780331134476 - Gloss Lamination